ENGLISH GRAMMAR
FOR SECONDARY SCHOOLS

ENGLISH GRAMMAR
FOR SECONDARY SCHOOLS

ADELAIDE MARY ABRAHAM

authorHOUSE®

AuthorHouse™
1663 Liberty Drive
Bloomington, IN 47403
www.authorhouse.com
Phone: 1-800-839-8640

Published by AuthorHouse   03/18/2013

ISBN: 978-1-4634-2709-2 (sc)
ISBN: 978-1-4634-2710-8 (e)

Any people depicted in stock imagery provided by Thinkstock are models, and such images are being used for illustrative purposes only.
Certain stock imagery © Thinkstock.

This book is printed on acid-free paper.

Because of the dynamic nature of the Internet, any web addresses or links contained in this book may have changed since publication and may no longer be valid. The views expressed in this work are solely those of the author and do not necessarily reflect the views of the publisher, and the publisher hereby disclaims any responsibility for them.

GYE NYAME

(Except God)

(Only God would make such wonders possible)

"With God, all things are possible"

Mark 10:27

This book was compiled by Adelaide Mary Abraham who taught Language Arts for many years in the U.S. Adelaide Mary Abraham has a B.A. in English and has almost completed a Master's in the same field.

Acknowledgements

Many thanks to Mrs. Gale Lewis who read the proof at its very inception and who encouraged me. Mrs. Lewis is the Principal at Gompers Elementary School. Also my sincere thanks to L. Marie Michelle Lumpkin, who was so kind to edit this book. Mrs. Lumpkin teaches Language Arts at Frank Murphy Middle School. Mrs. Lumpkin is also an adjunct Professor at Wayne County Community College in Detroit, Michigan.

Again, my heartfelt thanks to Mrs. Patricia Holmes, who took the time to correct the entire work at such short notice. Mrs. Holmes is the head of the English Department at Redford High School in Redford, Michigan.

It's quite unique to see a Grammar Book which is thematically structured! Excellent job.

Patricia Holmes

The *English Grammar for Secondary Schools* and the *Teacher's Edition High School English* are thorough and well thought out.

Bonnie Dobkin
VP & Editorial Director
McDougal Littell

This book is excellent and very well done.

Dr. Francis K. Buah

SUBJECTS, PREDICATES, AND SENTENCES

Firstly, in this lesson, we are going to learn about the different kinds of sentences, that we use in our everyday speech and writing. Secondly, we are going to learn about the two main parts of a sentence namely, subject and predicate.

FOUR KINDS OF SENTENCES

People express themselves or ideas by putting a group of words together to make sense. This we call a sentence. A sentence is a group of words that makes a complete sense. Different kinds of sentences express different kinds of ideas. We express ourselves by means of sentences, meaning putting words together as a group to make sense. Some sentences simply give information, some ask questions, some give command, or express some feelings. There are four kinds of sentences: They are informative, interrogative, imperative and exclamatory.

An informative sentence makes a statement and ends with a period.

I love to sing African songs.

An interrogative sentence asks a question and ends with a question mark.

Does nature replenish itself?

An imperative sentence gives a command and ends with a period.

Go to the schools and help discipline the students.

An exclamatory sentence expresses strong feelings, and ends with an exclamatory mark!

What an extraordinary party this has been!

1

EXERCISES

A. Copy out each sentence. Add the punctuation mark at the end of each sentence. Indicate whether the sentence is informative, interrogative, imperative, or exclamatory.

1. Meteorologists study the weather patterns
2. Do they predict the weather
3. What lovely weather it has been today
4. Let's hear your prediction about tomorrow's weather
5. You should listen to the weather to help plan for the day

B. Copy out each sentence. Add the correct punctuation. Then indicate whether the sentence is informative, interrogative, exclamatory or imperative.

6. That lady always wears a funny hat
7. It is likely that it will rain tonight
8. Tell me if you read any of Shakespeare's comedies
9. Keats wrote most of my favorite poems
10. What a character that man was

REINFORCEMENT: WRITING SENTENCES

Write ten sentences about one of the topics below making use of the informative, interrogative, imperative, and exclamatory sentences.

1. Describe any interesting narrative you have read.
2. Imagine you are a novelist. Write five sentences about one of your stories or novels.

SENTENCES AND SENTENCE FRAGMENTS

A sentence is a group of words that makes sense. A sentence fragment is a group of words that expresses only a partial thought.

Happy faces: They all have happy faces today because of the lovely weather.

Plenty of hay: There is plenty of hay to feed the animals during winter.

The group of words: happy faces, plenty of hay, do not make sense because they express only part of a thought. They are therefore known as sentence fragments. The group of words on the right makes complete sense. Each group of words therefore is a sentence.

A sentence is a group of words that makes a complete thought.

A sentence fragment is a group of words that does not make sense because it is only part of a sentence.

Every sentence is divided into two parts. One part is the complete subject. The other part is the complete predicate.

The complete subject, also known as the subject part of a sentence, names whom or what the sentence is talking about.

The complete predicate, or the predicate part, talks about what the subject is doing or is like. The complete predicate does not limit itself to one word.

Young teachers	*are in demand.*
Young teachers	*are scarce.*

3

In the first sentence, the complete subject is _teachers_ in the gray box. It tells what the sentence is about. The complete predicate, 'are in demand' in the white box talks about the subject. Both parts joined together make sense, whereas each part by itself does not.

In the second sentence, _young teachers_ in the gray box is the complete subject; it describes what the subject is about. The complete predicate _are scarce_ in the white box talks about the subject.

EXERCISES

A. Indicate whether each group of words is a sentence or sentence fragment.

1. God created the world in seven days.
2. Under the greenwood tree.
3. Many people enjoy the spring weather.
4. Plants and flowers begin to grow in the spring.
5. There are twelve months in a year.
6. Living in good climate.
7. Sharing interesting ideas.
8. Looking forward to warm weather.
9. It is always wise to finish school.
10. High aspirations will always put you to the top.

B. Copy out each group of words that form a complete sentence. Underline the complete subject once and the complete predicate twice. Write fragment if the group of words is not a complete sentence.

11. Men as well as animals depend on the forest.
12. The forest provides food and wood for man.
13. The forest provides food and shelter for animals.
14. The wood from the forest has many uses.
15. The carpenter depends on the wood for his livelihood.
16. Many household items are made of wood.
17. All furniture is made of wood.
18. Some saucepan handles and wooden spoons are made of wood.
19. The gardener depends on the wood, too.
20. Many garden tools are made of wood.

REINFORCEMENT: WRITING SENTENCES

Write ten sentences on one of the following topics.

1. The timber industry.
2. The carpenter and his shop.

COMPLETE AND SIMPLE SUBJECTS

Below are two sentences. In each sentence, the complete subject will appear in a gray box. Also the main word in each complete subject will be underlined.

Dedicated nurses	*are in great demand.*
Nurses with years of experience	*are scarce.*

The complete subject or main words in both sentences is the word *nurses*.
The main word or group of words of a complete subject is known as the <u>simple subject</u>.
The simple subject may be a noun or pronoun.
A noun is the name of a person, place, thing or idea.
A pronoun takes the place of a noun.

The simple subject is the main word or a collection of words in the complete subject

In some sentences, the <u>simple subject</u> forms the complete subject.

Nurses	*take care of patients.*

Care should be taken in the case of interrogative sentence.
In an interrogative sentence, the complete subject often precedes the first word in the sentence, for example:

1. Do <u>parents</u> in Africa allow teachers to discipline their children?
2. Do <u>children</u> respect their teachers?

The best way to find the subject of an interrogative sentence is to reword it into an informative sentence.

1. <u>Parents</u> in Africa do allow teachers to discipline their children.
2. <u>Children</u> do respect their teachers in Africa.

In an imperative sentence someone usually commands you to do something.
Assuming someone says to you. "Be on time" the subject part of the sentence in this case is the word 'you'. 'You,' therefore, is the "understood" subject part in an imperative sentence.

EXERCISES

A.   Copy out each sentence. Underline the complete subject once and underline the simple subject twice.

1.   Able farmers produce abundant crops.
2.   Their hard work always pays off.
3.   Careful observation of the weather helps a great deal.
4.   Good environment is a big asset.
5.   Many farmers are acquainted with the weather patterns in their environment.

B.   Copy out each sentence. Draw one line under the complete subject, and draw two lines under the simple subject. Reword the sentence in the case of an imperative sentence by writing the word 'you' to indicate the understood subject in an imperative sentence.

6.   Cocoa production is in the Ashanti Region.
7.   Cocoa farmers dedicate all their lives on the farm.
8.   Their main aim is to export their product.
9.   The cocoa beans are dried and shipped.
10. The Ashanti farmers are proud of their work.

REINFORCEMENT: WRITING SENTENCES

1.   Write ten sentences identifying the complete subject and the simple subject in each sentence.
2.   Write a short paper underlining five complete subjects and five simple subjects.

COMPLETE AND SIMPLE PREDICATES

Below are two sentences showing the complete predicate.

| Doctors | play a big role in society. |

| They | are the life of a nation. |

'*Play a big role in society*' and '*are the life of a nation*' are the complete predicate in these two sentences.

Play and *are* show the main words in the two complete predicates.

The main word or group of words in the complete predicate is known as the simple predicate.

The simple predicate has another name, *the verb.*

> The simple predicate has the main word or group of words in the complete predicate.

An interrogative sentence in most cases begins with part of the predicate. The rest of the predicate part will appear at the end of the sentence after the subject.

| Do | children | change during adolescence? |

The best way to find the predicate part of an interrogative sentence is to reword it as an informative sentence.

| Children | do change during adolescence. |

In an imperative sentence someone is asking somebody to do something. The understood subject therefore, in this sentence is 'you'. The predicate part is the command itself, or what the person really asks you to do. Assuming, *your mama asks you to wash the dishes; Your mama* really means, "*You*" wash the dishes.

Wash the dishes is the complete predicate and wash the (verb) is the simple predicate.
In the case where sentences begin with *there is* and *there are*, here the predicate part starts
the sentence.

| There are | plants and flowers. | Plants and flowers | are there. |

The complete predicate is '*are there*' and the simple predicate is '*are*'.

EXERCISES

A. Copy out each sentence. Draw a line under the complete predicate and two lines under simple predicate.

1. Scientists rely on hypothesis for their findings.
2. Geologists do excavations to find out about rock formations.
3. Anthropologists study man in its widest sense.
4. Botanists study all about plants.
5. Erosion plays a great part on the earth's surface.
6. Zoologists study animal life.
7. Ecologists study animal population.
8. Metaphysics is the science, which investigates the first principles of nature and thought.

B. Copy out each sentence. Draw one line under the complete predicate of the sentence and two lines under the simple predicate. Reword the sentence if necessary.

9. Do children change during adolescence?
10. Parents in Africa expect their children to obey their teachers.
11. Do students obey their teachers in Africa?
12. Observe the weather patterns for this week.
13. Does the manager plan the shift according to the weather?
14. People expect good weather in the spring.
15. The climate in Ghana is nearly always over 70 degrees Fahrenheit.
16. In Ghana, we do have torrential rainfall in May, June, and July.

REINFORCEMENT: WRITING SENTENCES

1. Write ten sentences identifying the complete predicate and the simple predicate.
2. Describe the climate in your region and explain how it affects people's lives.

COMPOUND SUBJECTS AND PREDICATES

In some cases, a sentence may have more than one simple subject, more than one simple predicate or more than either of the two. The sentence is then said to have a compound subject or predicate.

A compound subject, has two or more simple subjects while sharing the same predicate. The subjects are joined by 'and' or 'or'.

The following are two sentences; each sentence containing a compound subject.

Administrators and teachers	*meet once a week.*
Both administrators and teachers	*meet once a week.*

When the two simple subjects are joined by <u>*and*</u> or by <u>*both*</u> . . . <u>*and*</u>, the compound subject must be plural. You must use the plural form of the verb to agree with this plural compound subject.

Compound subjects may be singular; when simple subjects are joined by <u>*or*</u> the compound subject may be singular or plural.

The foreman or a worker	*distributes the leaflets.*
The foreman or his workers	*distribute the leaflets.*

In the two sentences above, the predicate must agree with the *closer* simple subject—<u>*worker*</u> is the closer subject in the first sentence and the verb <u>*distributes*</u> agrees with the singular subject.

Some sentences have more than one predicate.

In the second sentence '*workers*' is the closer subject, and the verb '*distribute*' must agree with the plural subject.

A compound predicate has two or more simple predicates and share the same subject. The simple subjects are joined by *and* or *or*.

| *Scientists* | *hypothesize and predict a scientific outcome.* |

Hypothesize and *predict* are the simple predicates or verbs in the compound predicate. The plural noun *scientists* is the subject of both verbs. Both verbs agree with the plural noun, which is the subject.

EXERCISES

A. Copy out each sentence. Write compound subject if the subject of the sentence is compound. Underline each simple subject once. Write compound predicate if the predicate of the sentence is compound. Then underline each simple predicate twice.

1. Boys and girls work in restaurants.
2. Men and women care for their young ones.
3. Birds and animals live in our environment.
4. Scientists observe and hypothesize.
5. Astronomers study and predict the future.
6. Erosion destroys and lays waste the land.

B. Fill in the blanks with the correct verb or verbs and underline the verbs.

7. Plants _____ chlorophyll by means of photosynthesis. (make, makes)
8. Playing with water and electricity may _____ injury. (cause, causes)
9. Birds and some animals _____ with pollination. (help, helps)
10. Most animals _____ in the winter. (hibernate, hibernates)

REINFORCEMENT: WRITING SENTENCES

Write on a topic about animals in our environment using compound subjects and compound predicate.
Write about animal hibernation during the winter.

COMPOUND SENTENCES

A simple sentence is a sentence with one subject part and one predicate part.
A simple sentence may have one subject part and one predicate part. A sentence may also have both compound subjects and a compound predicate.

Mary and Agnes		**work together.**
They		**research and study works of art.**

One may have to join or combine two related ideas into one longer sentence to form a compound sentence. In this case, you may use a coordinating conjunction to join two simple sentences: *and, or,* or *but.*
A compound sentence is a sentence that has two or more simple sentences joined by a coordinating conjunction.
A compound sentence may have two complete subjects and two predicates.

One scientist	**hypothesizes on nature**	**but**	**his ideas**

are not convincing.

Some conjunctions are paired together. They are known as correlative conjunctions: *either . . . or/and/neither . . . nor.* They are used to connect words or groups of words.
Either the students do their homework, or suffer the consequences thereof.

There is usually a comma before a conjunction to separate the two parts of a compound sentence. Where the two parts of a compound sentence already has two commas, one may use a semi-colon (;) to separate the two parts

Doctors	*study different parts of the body;*

the brain, the intestines, and the nerves;	*and*	*they do research to help them in their work.*

Doctors	*discuss research data with other doctors;*	*they*

share ideas.

EXERCISES

A. Here are some sentences; some are compound sentences while others are simple sentences with compound subjects or compound predicates. Write down each sentence and identify the kind of sentence.

1. African fishermen study the weather, and their search helps them a great deal.
2. They eat and sell what they have caught for the day.
3. They fish everyday of the week but rest on Tuesdays.
4. The fishermen weave their nets, and build their own boats.
5. They are seen at times mending their nets and painting their boats.
6. Some fishermen will just fish, and market women will buy off their whole catch and sell them in the market.

B. Copy out each sentence. Say whether it is a simple sentence or a compound sentence. Draw one line under each subject, if the sentence has compound subject. Draw two lines under each verb, if the sentence has a compound predicate.

7. Teachers teach children, and their hard work makes useful citizens.
8. Doctors diagnose and operate on patients daily.
9. They are putting structures everywhere, but they must be durable.
10. Are the parents going to find a better way to control their children or are they going to bear the consequences?

REINFORCEMENT: WRITING SENTENCES:

Write ten compound sentences on one of the following topics.

1. Describe a scene at the beach with fishermen and market women.
2. Describe the fisherman at the sea.

REVIEW

FOUR KINDS OF SENTENCES

A. Copy out each sentence and write the necessary punctuation. Then say whether the sentence is informative, interrogative, imperative or exclamatory sentence.

1. You shall not kill
2. Do you love to go to school
3. I love to go to school
4. What an extraordinary story
5. Please be sure you turn in your homework
6. What a wonderful day this has been
7. Do you ever study after school

SENTENCE AND SENTENCE FRAGMENTS

B. Write each group of words that form a complete sentence. Underline the complete subject once and the complete predicate twice. If the group of words is not a complete sentence, write fragment.

8. Birds flocking together.
9. Most parents try their best for their children.
10. The laborer is worthy of his hire.
11. Looking forward to win.
12. Bits and pieces.
13. How lucky it is to be here.
14. I shall love to visit my aunt in the summer.

Young Ghanaian women with Fishermen at sea.

Ghanaian Fishermen With Their Boats At The Seashore

COMPLETE AND SIMPLE SUBJECTS

C. Write each sentence. If interrogative change into informative. Then draw a line under the complete subject of the sentence. Circle the simple subject. Write the understood word 'You' for an imperative sentence.

15. Come to the ball game.
16. Please shut the door.
17. A large crater fell into space.
18. Have you 6th graders studied about the famous scientist Albert Einstein?
19. We 6th graders have studied about the famous scientist Albert Einstein.
20. The Ministry of Education will supply all you need.

COMPLETE AND SIMPLE PREDICATES

D. Copy out each sentence, rewording interrogative sentence as informative sentence if necessary. Then, draw one line under the complete predicate of the sentence. Circle the simple predicate.

21. Many fishermen fish and provide food for us.
22. Able farmers plant different kinds of crops for consumption.
23. Do birds and animals cause pollination?
24. Birds and animals do cause pollination.

COMPOUND SUBJECTS AND PREDICATES

E.   Fill in the blanks with the correct verb form.

25. Children and adults _____ to the library everyday. (go, goes)
26. Labor officers _____ hard and _____ their best. (works, work), (tries, try)
27. Cocoa farmers _____ relentlessly so they can export their crop. (labors, labor)

COMPOUND SENTENCES

F.   Copy out each sentence. Identify whether it is a simple sentence or a compound sentence. If the sentence has a compound subject, identify it by drawing a line under each simple subject. If the sentence has a compound predicate, draw a double line under each simple predicate. Then draw a line between the two simple sentences.

28. Many students do well in school; they also have time for other activities.
29. Children in Africa are anxious to go to school; but the books and materials are lacking.
30. In good season, farmers sow crops in abundance, and harvest them in August.
31. Scientists and astronomers work together trying to provide answers; they will some day discover all they are searching for.
32. Some people have wonderful ideas; they fail to implement them.

NOUNS

In this lesson, we are going to learn about different kinds of nouns, the words we employ to name persons, places, things and ideas.

> A noun is the name of a person, place, thing or idea.

KINDS OF NOUNS

Many nouns name things that are tangible meaning things that you can touch; book, table, chair, pencil or ruler.

Other nouns are called abstract nouns because they cannot be seen or touched; examples are courage, truth, feelings and ideas.

All the tangible nouns named above are common nouns. There are proper nouns too.

> A proper noun is a noun that names a specific person, place, thing or idea.

A noun that names a specific person, place or thing, or idea is called a proper noun. Your name, names of cities, towns, rivers, street names, title of books, etc. are all proper nouns. The first letters of proper nouns are capitalized. Ghana, Accra, Cape Coast, Elmina, Kumasi, Holy Child School, Akosombo River, Britain, United States, Europe, California, Dade Street.

POSSESSIVE NOUNS

Possessive nouns show ownership. They can be singular or plural.

John owns a musical instrument.

John's instrument is new.

John is a singular proper noun.

The word *John's* is a singular possessive noun.

The statue has a magnificent face.

The statue's face is magnificent.

The word statue's with the apostrophe 's also indicates a possessive noun. Both John's and statue's are singular possessive nouns.

To form most possessive singular nouns add an apostrophe 's. If the noun is plural and does not end in s, add 's.

Men—men's

Women—women's

People—people's

TO FORM THE PLURAL POSSESSIVE NOUNS:

If the plural noun ends in s, just add an apostrophe.

The girls have different exercise books.

The girls' exercise books are different.

POSSESSIVE NOUNS

Possessive nouns show ownership. They show what one owns.

Paul owns a large shop.

Paul's shop is large.

Paul is a singular proper noun. The word Paul's is a singular possessive noun.

The board has a beautiful top.

The board's top is beautiful.

The word board is a singular common noun. The word board's with the apostrophe 's indicates a possessive noun. Both Paul's and board's are singular possessive nouns.

> **To form most possessive singular nouns add an apostrophe and—s, ('s).**

Below are some examples of singular nouns and their possessive forms.

A boy	—	*a boy's toy*
A rabbit	—	*a rabbit's tail*
A girl	—	*a girl's dress*
My teacher	—	*my teacher's class*
Doctor	—	*doctor's*
Hero	—	*hero's*
Diary	—	*diary's*

Note that when a singular noun already ends with an—s, you still have to add ('s) to form the possessive.

Jesus Miracle Plays	—	*Jesus' Miracle plays.*
Mrs. Masters	—	*Mrs. Masters's cook book.*

PLURAL POSSESSIVE NOUNS

> **To form the possessive of most plural nouns that end in—s, add an apostrophe (').**
> **To form the possessive of plural nouns that do not end in—s, add an apostrophe—s ('s).**

Plural nouns and their possessive forms:

men	—	*men's uniforms*
women	—	*women's apparel*
boys	—	*boys' attire*

Study the following list:

Plural Nouns	Plural Possessive Nouns
Doctors	Doctors'
Heroes	Heroes'
Diaries	Diaries'

EXERCISES

A.   Give the possessive forms of the underlined.

<u>Mary</u> favorite song
<u>Children</u> outfit
<u>Country</u> code
<u>Men</u> socks
<u>Drivers</u> manual
<u>Shakespeare</u> sonnets

B.   Copy out each sentence and put the right apostrophe in the right place.

1. Many of Keats poems are didactic.
2. One of Agnes sons goes to Redford High School.
3. People homes are very well painted nowadays.
4. The school office is located at the far end corner.
5. The children teacher will be back soon.
6. I hear tomorrow weather will be better.
7. One of Mike shoelaces is missing.
8. Old people homes are rented out all year round.
9. The recent storm destroyed many citizens homes.
10. She loves to buy from the popular <u>men</u> stores.

REINFORCEMENT: WRITING SENTENCES

Write ten sentences using singular or plural possessive forms on one of the following.

1. The rainy season in West Africa.
2. How farmers harvest their crops.

A COLLECTIVE NOUN IS MADE UP OF A GROUP OF PEOPLE OR THINGS

A group of people

A committee of people

A shoal of fish

A team of players

A herd of cattle

A swarm of bees

A flock of birds

Collective nouns may be singular or plural. Nouns and verbs must always agree in the sentences. When the subject of the sentence is singular, the verb of the sentence should also be in the singular formation. If the subject of the sentence is plural, the verb in the sentence should also be plural thus the verb agreeing with the subject.

Collective nouns may pose specific agreement problems. Every collective noun may have a singular or a plural meaning. When speaking about a group as a unit, the noun should have a singular meaning. When referring to the individual members of the group, the noun must have a plural meaning.

The entire flock charged into the field through the gate. (a unit, singular)

The flock enters by different gates. (individual members, plural)

The team decides on its proposal. (a unit, singular)

The team decided on their separate proposals. (plural)

EXERCISES

A. Copy out each sentence, and underline the collective noun. Then indicate whether the collective noun is singular or plural.

1. A team of players arrives from different countries.
2. Each team is determined to win.
3. The flock of birds took to flight as we approached the field.
4. The committee finally agrees with a unanimous decision.
5. The committee from different African nations arrived with one important concern.
6. The class came with different ideas concerning their school.
7. My class prepares to play hockey with another school.

B. Copy out each sentence and underline the collective noun. Write plural for the plural collective noun and singular for the singular collective noun.

1. I am a member of the choir that sings at Christmas at Holy Cross Church.
2. The choir sings a medley of songs for the occasion.
3. Our favorite soccer team plays tonight.
4. The football team in our area faces the camera today.
5. The whole class meets after church on Sunday for refreshment.
6. The School Board meets on Friday.
7. A fleet of ships leaves the harbor at dawn for our hometown.
8. The crowd cheered with such a loud noise.
9. The crowd leaves at different times.

REINFORCEMENT: WRITING SENTENCES

Write ten sentences on one of the following topics using collective nouns.

1. Describe an annual concert held at the end of the school year.
2. Describe a football match held at your school.

APPOSITIVES

A noun, when it is written next to another noun, identifies or adds further information about that noun.

Michelangelo, a painter, made an important contribution to art and sculpture.

An appositive, therefore, is a noun that is placed next to another noun in order to give extra information about that noun.

Michelangelo, an Italian artist, made a great contribution to art and sculpture.

The noun "artist" still identifies Michelangelo the same way "the painter" did in the first sentence. In the second sentence, however, the word Italian is used to further describe the artist. Together the words *an Italian* and *painter* form an appositive phrase that identifies Michelangelo.

The appositive phrase may be at the beginning, middle or at the end of the sentence. (as long as it is near the noun it identifies) A comma is used after the appositive if it appears at the beginning and end of a sentence. Notice that two commas set off the appositives apart in the middle of the sentence.

EXERCISES

A. Copy out each sentence. Identify each appositive or appositive phrase. Circle the noun that the appositive identifies, adding commas where necessary.

1. Leonardo da Vinci a fifteen century Italian had many talents.
2. Da Vinci an Italian artist painted extraordinary pictures that hang today in most famous galleries.
3. In Florence a city in Italy Da Vinci painted his famous Mona Lisa.
4. A scientist and an engineer Da Vinci wrote many papers.
5. Da Vinci this extraordinary artist painted the Lord's Last Supper.

B. Copy out each sentence. Underline the appositive or the appositive phrase. Circle the noun that the appositive is referring to.

1. Prince Henry a famous Portuguese was the first to explore the Eastern route to the Indies.
2. Henry also known as the Navigator tried to convert the people of Asia to Christianity.
3. Prince Henry the navigator also founded one of the most unique training schools of his time which was a college of seamen, ship builders and navigators.
4. Prince Henry this extraordinary prince trained the finest Portuguese himself.

REINFORCEMENT: WRITING SENTENCES

1. Write about a unique individual you have read about using five appositive phrases.
2. Write about a scientist you have studied using five appositive phrases.

REVIEW

A. KINDS OF NOUNS

Identify the nouns in each sentence below. Say whether they are common nouns or proper nouns by writing the correct name above the nouns. Then state whether each noun is concrete or abstract noun.

Common/concrete Common/concrete abstract
Example: The __farmer__ tilted his __plots__ with great __enthusiasm__.

1. The children played happily at the game.
2. The scientist explained his ideas thoroughly.
3. Mary showed her daughter how to play the game.
4. Old people have developed a way to spend their time.
5. The archeologist discovered a strategy to fulfill his dreams.

B. POSSESSIVE NOUNS

Write the correct possessive nouns for the following.

Woman	Boy	Clerk
Fan	Man	Mice
Jesus	Family	Wives
Guest	People	Spencer
Doctor	Tuesday	Janice

C. Copy out each sentence, putting the correct apostrophe in the right place. Then identify both the singular possessive noun and the plural possessive noun.

1. __Vladimin Zworkin__ television was the first practical television to make __its__ way into the market.
2. __Today__ television carried both __adult__ and __children__ programs.
3. __Teacher__ collective effort always pays off.
4. There are many __doctor__ assistants working outside of the hospital.
5. __Worker__ compensation needs to be upgraded.
6. __Scientists__ past effort is improving the future scientific discovery.

D. Copy out each sentence using the correct word in the parentheses to fill in the blanks. Write whether the word is a singular noun or a plural noun. Also indicate if the word is plural possessive noun.

1. We have no idea of these _____ owner. (books', books)
2. Galileo Galilei positioned his telescope at the _____ orbit. (planets, planet's)
3. Galileo's _____ set the record straight. (discoveries, discovery's)
4. We cannot tell which _____ autograph this is. (man's, man)
5. I wonder whose _____ are on the shelf. (books, book's)
6. The _____ dresses are ready. (children, children's)

E. Copy out each sentence, and underline the collective noun. Indicate whether the collective noun is plural or singular.

1. The committee decides the different winners.
2. The crowd surges forward each time there is a score.
3. She always has a good audience.
4. The Legion serves good food.
5. My club meets everyday.

F. Copy out each sentence, and then use the correct verb in parentheses to fill in the blanks.

1. A swarm of bees (bother, bothers) my roses.
2. A herd of cattle (push, pushes) through the gate.
3. A gang of rascals (face, faces) the judge.
4. A group of people (watch, watches) the parade every year.
5. A herd of cattle (rush, rushes) through the barnyard.

G. Copy out each sentence, and underline the appositive or appositive phrase. Add commas where necessary.

1. John Donne a seventeen century poet used the metaphysical tradition.
2. William Shakespeare who was Donne's contemporary employed like imagery in his work.
3. Tate another contemporary of Donne wrote explaining the sources and content of Donne's imagery.
4. Shakespeare who wrote a lot of comedies, tragedies, etc. is sometimes doubted as being the true author of his plays.

VERBS

In this lesson, you are going to learn about words that show action or tell what the subject of a sentence is doing or is like.

An action verb shows action or tells what the subject is doing.

1. *The kid <u>watches</u> television everyday.*
2. *The man <u>works</u> at the plant.*

Underline the action verbs in the following sentences.

The Ashanti Kotoko team arrived eagerly to play their counterpart. They came with their coach who addressed them as to how to play the game. Encouraging them, the coach had strengthened his team to strive to win the game. This team therefore played brilliantly, and won. The Ashanti Kotoko team was cheered and honored, and are still respected up to this day.

The words honored, strengthened and respected express mental activity.
Has, have and had are action verbs, too, when they name what belongs to the subject of the sentence.

REINFORCEMENT: WRITING SENTENCES

1. Write ten sentences about action verbs.
2. Use ten action verbs in sentences.

Copy out each sentence. Underline the action verbs and say whether they express physical or mental action.

1. Holy Child Secondary school had a Hockey team.
2. We played against other girls' high schools.
3. We always practiced hard before the game.
4. We met every afternoon for practice.
5. The team won a number of trophies.
6. The netball game led to the creation of another game.
7. Every game had its rules.
8. It was important that everyone memorized the rules.

REINFORCEMENT: WRITING SENTENCES

Write ten sentences about one of the following.

1. My favorite sport.
2. Imagine that your school is competing in a game. Write about how your school did.

DIRECT OBJECTS, TRANSITIVE AND INTRANSITIVE VERBS

We learned that every sentence has two parts, the subject part and the predicate part.

In some sentences, there is only one action verb that makes up the predicate part.

| *The teacher* | teaches | *the students* | listen. |

Usually sentences are more elaborate. The predicate part often shows who or what receives the action of the verb.

| *The teacher* | *teaches the play.* |

| *The students* | *listen to Ms. Tate.* |

In the two sentences above, *play* and *Ms. Tate* receive the action of the verbs *teaches* and *listen*. They answer the question what? or whom? They are known as direct objects of verbs.

> **The direct object of a verb receives the action of the verb. It answers the question whom? or what? after an action verb.**

Some sentences have compound direct objects. In other words, more than one direct object.

| *We* | *met Mary and Rosa at the store.* |

| *The spectators* | *brought chairs and stools along.* |

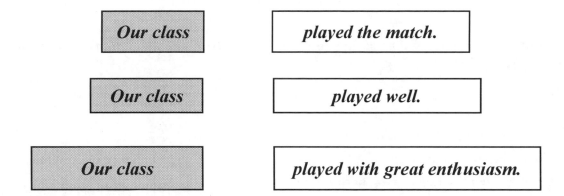

In the first sentence above, <u>match</u> is the direct object because it answers the question what? after the verb played. In the second and third sentences <u>well</u> and <u>with great enthusiasm</u> do not answer the question whom? or what? after the verb played. Therefore they are not direct objects. They are known as intransitive verbs.

A transitive verb has a direct object. An intransitive verb is a verb that does not have a direct object.

EXERCISES

Copy out each sentence and underline the action verb; then indicate if the verb is transitive or intransitive.

1. Joe saw the captain.
2. The carpenter fixed the door.
3. The children played cards.
4. A girl carried the flag during her hometown festival.

Copy out each sentence and underline each verb. Indicate whether it is transitive or intransitive. If it is transitive, circle the direct object.

1. Ann gave her mother the message.
2. Joseph explained the meaning of the passage.
3. Our teacher bought us some pizza.
4. The actors studied their script.
5. The ship finally sailed away.
6. The children come to play after school.
7. My friend arrived last night.
8. We quickly invited our mother.
9. Some members came late.
10. Most workers are always on time.
11. Your friend called.

REINFORCEMENT: WRITING SENTENCES

Write ten sentences on one of the following topics, employing direct objects in each sentence.

1. Write about the forest and how it benefits mankind.
2. Write about the new technology and the impact it is having in today's world.

LINKING VERBS, PREDICATE, NOUNS AND PREDICATE ADJECTIVES

Unlike action verbs that tell us what the subject does, linking verbs do not tell us what the subject of a sentence does. Rather, they say what the subject is or is like.

| *François* | is a carpenter. | Joseph | was unique. |

The *is* in the first sentence and the *was* in the second sentence are verbs, but they do not show action. They each link the subject to a word in the predicate. The word *carpenter* tells what the subject *François* is, and the word *unique* tells what the subject *Joseph was* like.

> *A linking verb is a verb that links or joins the subject part with a noun or adjective in the predicate part. It tells what the subject is or is like.*

If the word in the predicate is a noun, it tells what the subject is.
The word that follows a linking verb may be a noun, or an adjective. A noun that follows a linking verb is known as predicate noun.

Kate is a seamstress.

> *A predicate adjective is an adjective that follows a linking verb. It describes the subject by telling what it is like.*

The following are some examples of linking verbs.
The forms of the verb 'be' (is, am, are, was, were, being, been) and the verbs seems, feels, taste, sound, appear, smell, grow, look, become, and turn. Many of these verbs can be used as action verbs.

She grows restless. (linking verb)   *The African farmer grows corn. (action verb).*
She smells nice. (linking verb)She smells roses. (action verb)

EXERCISES

A. Copy out each sentence and underline each verb. Differentiate between the action verb and the linking verb. If the sentence contains a linking verb, show whether it is followed by a predicate noun or a predicate adjective.

1. That athlete runs very fast.
2. The weather looks dull.
3. My neighbor plays hockey.
4. Some students work hard.
5. She is a good neighbor.

B. Underline each verb in every sentence. State whether it is an action verb or a linking verb.

1. The boy jumped over the ladder.
2. These children seem happy to me.
3. Mary is a good choice for the role.
4. He sounds serious.

REINFORCEMENT: WRITING SENTENCES

Write ten sentences on one of the following using a different kind of linking verb in each sentence.

1. A busy market in your hometown.
2. A busy thoroughfare.

VERBS WITH INDIRECT OBJECTS

We have learned that linking verbs join the subject part of a sentence with nouns or adjectives in the predicate part. We have also learned that if the word in the predicate part is a noun, it is called a predicate noun. A predicate noun is a noun that follows a linking verb. It tells what the subject is.

The sentence below shows a predicate noun.

He was their best <u>umpire or referee</u> this year.

In most cases, action verbs, too, are followed by nouns and pronouns. Nouns or pronouns that answer the question whom? or what? after an action verb are known as direct objects. Notice the direct objects in the following sentences.

Joseph Andrew threw the <u>ball</u>.
Joseph led his <u>class</u> to success once again.

It is likely that two kinds of objects will follow an action verb. The object that <u>directly receives the action is known as</u>, direct object. Another object known as the <u>Indirect Object</u> may also follow the verb. An indirect object shows to whom or for whom the action is done.

Joseph shows his <u>class</u> interesting maneuvering.
The star football player gives my <u>friend</u> a handshake.

The direct object in the first sentence is <u>class</u>. The Indirect Object is <u>friend</u>.

> *The indirect object of a verb answers the question to whom? Or for whom?. The action is done.*

There are two easy ways to help recognize indirect objects. First, the indirect object always comes before a direct object. Second, one can add the preposition to or for before the indirect object and change its position.

The teacher gives the <u>children</u> reading books.

The teacher gives the reading books <u>to the children</u>.

In the first sentence, <u>children</u> is the indirect objects. Firstly, it comes before the direct object. Secondly, its position can be changed, thereby following the preposition *to*.

EXERCISES

A. Copy out each sentence. Then indicate whether each underlined noun in the predicate part is a predicate noun, direct object, or indirect object.

1. Mr. Thomas scores for his <u>team</u> some <u>marks</u> right at the start.
2. The man who is a quarterback is a <u>student</u>.
3. Some of the <u>players</u> were students.
4. Matthew threw the <u>batter</u> a <u>hard ball</u>.

B. Copy out each sentence, and underline each verb twice. Indicate whether it is a linking verb or an action verb. Then indicate whether each underlined word in the predicate part is a predicate noun, a direct object or an indirect object.

1. Ann gave her mother the message.
2. Those children were friends at the beginning of the school year.
3. The instructor gave the students a new assignment.
4. Mrs. Smith is the new gym teacher.
5. Joseph showed his teammates new tricks.
6. The referee gives the players badges.
7. A friend was the reporter.

REINFORCEMENT: WRITING SENTENCES

Write ten sentences on one of the following topics using indirect object in each sentence.

1. A match at the end of the school year.
2. An interview with the referee.

PRESENT, PAST AND FUTURE TENSE

In English grammar, there are three simple tenses: past tense, present tense and future tense. A verb can indicate the past, present or future time or tell what time the action is really taking place.

These changes in form are called tenses.

> The present tense of a verb states that an action is taking place now.

How to form the present tense.

Present Tense	
SINGULAR	*PLURAL*
I play	*We play*
You play	*You play*
He, she, it plays	*They play*

The past tense for most verbs are formed by adding—ed to the present verb.

Present Tense	Past Tense
Play	Played
Dance	Danced
Wash	Washed
Jump	Jumped

The future tense shows an action that will take place in the future.

The helping verb shall is sometimes used with the verb to form the future tense for the pronouns I and we.

Future Tense	
SINGULAR	**PLURAL**
I will (shall) swim	*We will swim*
You will swim	*You will swim*
He, she, it will swim	*They will swim*

EXERCISES

A. Copy out each sentence; underline the verb and state whether the verb is in the present, past or future tense.

1. William Wordsworth wrote didactic poems.
2. He showed some interesting incites into man's life.
3. His poem that really elevates me is his "Ode: Intimations to Immortality."
4. He is looked upon as one of the best romantic poets.

B. Copy out each sentence. Then fill in the blanks using the correct verb form in the parentheses.

1. William Wordsworth, though no longer alive is still greatly _____. (admired, admire)
2. He _____ an austere life. (lead, led)
3. Wordsworth, a great English Romantic poet and poet laureate, _____ a name for himself. (make, made)
4. He and his contemporary Samuel Taylor Coleridge _____ the English Romantic movement. (initiate, initiated)
5. Wordsworth _____ his lyrical ballads together with his friend Coleridge. (write, wrote)
6. Wordsworth's sister, Dorothy _____ to _____ light on her brother's work. (help, helped) (sheds, shed)
7. William Wordsworth _____ on nature the love that was lacking at home after his mother's death. (rely, relied)
8. On December 21, 1999, Wordsworth's sister, Dorothy _____ to the Lake District, at Grasmere, Westmorland. (return, returned)
9. Wordsworth _____ Mary Hutchinson who _____ him three children. (marry, married) (bear, bore)
10. Critics _____ of Wordsworth's marriage period as being the highest point in his life. (spoke, speak)

REINFORCEMENT: WRITING SENTENCES

Write ten sentences on one of the following topics.

1. My favorite poet.
2. My favorite poem.

PRINCIPAL PARTS, HELPING VERBS
AND VERB PHRASES

All tenses of a verb are formed from four principal parts and helping verbs. The following are four principal parts of a verb.

Present	Present Participle	Past	Past Participle
dance	dancing	danced	danced

The first principal part of a verb is the verb itself. In most cases, this part is used to form the present tense. The present participle is formed by adding—ing to the verb. The past and the past participle are formed by adding—ed to the verb. These two form the past and the past participle and are mostly the same for most verbs.

You have learned the future tense whereby you add the helping verb *will* or *shall* to form the future tense. In most cases the principal part of a verb is joined with a helping verb in a phrase in order to form other tenses.

A <u>helping verb</u> supports the main verb to show an action or make a statement. A verb phrase is made up of one or more helping verbs followed by a main verb. It names the action or describes the subject.

The people <u>are</u> hunting now. They <u>have</u> hunted here before.

The words, <u>are</u> and <u>have</u> above are helping verbs. <u>Hunting</u> and <u>hunted</u> are the main verbs. Most helping verbs are made from the verb (to) 'be' and 'have'. The present participle is usually used with the helping verb forms (to) 'be'. The past participle is usually used with the helping verb form 'have'.

To Be and the Present Participle		Have and the Past Participle	
I am dancing	I was dancing	I have danced	I had danced
You are dancing	You were dancing	You have danced	You had danced
He is dancing	He was dancing	He has danced	He had danced
She is dancing	She was dancing	She has danced	She had danced
It is dancing	It was dancing	It has danced	It had danced
We are dancing	We were dancing	We have danced	We had danced
You are dancing	You were dancing	You have danced	You had danced
They are dancing	They were dancing	They have danced	They had danced

EXERCISES

Copy out each sentence. Then fill in the blanks with the correct helping verb in the parentheses, and underline the verb phrase in the sentence.

1. The children _____ finished their work. (has, have)
2. Mary _____ finished cleaning the board. (has, is)
3. The people from other countries _____ helping the earthquake victims in Italy. (are, have)
4. The students who graduated from college _____ saying they did not waste time. (are, is)
5. The vendors in the market _____ packing up their wares. (are, have)

A. Fill in the blanks with the correct helping verb in the parentheses. Underline the verb phrase in the sentence, and draw a second line under the participle. Then indicate whether it is a present participle or a past participle.

1. The fishermen _____ weaving their nets. (were, had)
2. The students _____ playing soccer. (are, have)
3. Soccer games _____ becoming very popular. (are, have)
4. One of the soccer players _____ playing remarkably well. (is, has)
5. He _____ made a good impression in this game. (is, has)
6. One of the players' balls _____ missed the mark. (is, has)
7. Some players _____ used other means to win. (are, have)
8. The young player's mind _____ focusing solely on the game and her performance _____ improved. (is, has) (has, is)

REINFORCEMENT: WRITING SENTENCES

1. Write ten sentences using a verb phrase in each sentence.
2. Write a short story using as many verb phrases as you can and underline your verb phrases.

PRONOUNS

In this chapter, you are going to learn about pronouns. Pronouns are words that take the place of nouns in sentences. You will learn how to use different kinds of pronouns including those that show ownership and those that ask questions.

PERSONAL PRONOUNS

Some pronouns are in fact the subject of sentences.

Mary loves to sing. She always sings in the concert.

A subject pronoun can be used as a subject of a sentence.

A subject pronoun can be used as the subject of a sentence.

You can use a subject pronoun when you write a compound sentence that entails a noun and a pronoun.

Mary and I enjoy singing African songs.

Other pronouns are used as the object of verbs or prepositions.

African songs interest <u>Mary</u>. African songs interest <u>her</u>.

The new choir master introduced the national anthem to <u>us</u>.

An object pronoun is used as the object of a verb or of a preposition.

Use an object pronoun when you write a compound object that has a pronoun.
African chants and foreign songs appeal to <u>Joseph</u> and <u>her</u>.
Rosemary offered her notes to <u>her</u> and <u>me</u>.

Subject Pronouns	
I	We
You	*You*
She, he, it	*They*

Object Pronouns	
Me	*Us*
You	*You*
Her, him, it	*Them*

EXERCISES

A. **Copy out each sentence. Write the correct pronoun for each underlined word or words in the sentences.**

1. <u>Ancient writers</u> developed the tradition for writing legends.
2. <u>These writers</u> found interesting legends which had pagan origins.
3. Josiah studied the interpretation of <u>these legends</u>.
4. Legends of the past interest <u>Josiah</u>.
5. <u>Mary</u> analyzed the interpretations of one of the legends.
6. According to <u>Mary</u>, some fascinating legends can be traced back to antiquity.

B. **Copy out each sentence. Replace the underlined word or words with a pronoun and indicate whether the pronoun you used is a subject or object pronoun.**

7. <u>Our forefathers</u> developed many myths from olden days.
8. Some of the stories told by grandparents to <u>children</u> were myths.
9. A few of the <u>myths</u> sounded like true stories.
10. Others are just interesting fables told to both <u>young and old</u>.
11. <u>Ekua and Efua</u> loved to listen to such stories.
12. <u>Ekua</u> explained some of the stories to us.

REINFORCEMENT: WRITING SENTENCES

Write ten sentences using subject and object pronouns in a tale or a legend that you have read.

1. Underline the subject and object pronouns.
2. Create your own myth story.

PRONOUNS AND ANTECEDENTS

When a pronoun refers to the noun or a group of words, the noun or group of words that a pronoun refers to is known as its antecedent. When using a pronoun, make sure it refers to its antecedent. Be careful about the pronoun "they." Notice the following:

They have many reference books on hand at the desk.

It is not very clear to whom the word "they" refers to. You could correct the sentence by saying:

Many reference books are on hand at the desk.

Make sure each pronoun agrees with its antecedent in gender (masculine-male; feminine-female; neuter-nouns naming things-singular/plural).

The event is ceremonious. I love <u>it</u>.

Mary and Michelle are very good singers. <u>They</u> are sopranos.

The audience is watching Mary attentively. <u>They</u> are watching <u>her</u> with admiration.

In the first pair of sentences, "<u>*it*</u>" also agrees with <u>*the event*</u>.

In the second pair of sentences, the word "<u>*they*</u>" agrees with <u>*Mary and Michelle*</u>.

In the third pair of sentences, the word "<u>*they*</u>" agrees with <u>*the audience*</u> and "<u>*her*</u>" agrees with <u>*Mary*</u>.

EXAMPLES

My friend is a professor. <u>She</u> wrote a book on the modern woman.

My cousin is a king in Africa. <u>He</u> taught in one of the universities in Massachussetts.

The students loved my cousin. <u>They</u> were different nationalities.

Maya Angelou is a friend of the family. <u>She</u> is now one of the leading American writers.

EXERCISES

A. Fill in the blanks with the correct pronoun in the parentheses.

1. _____ and Robert told the audience about Greek Philosophers. (she, her)
2. My friend told my sister and _____ about bird watchers. (I, me)
3. _____ were the leaders of both hockey teams respectively. (they, them)
4. Grace and _____ tried to understand the passage. (I, me)
5. My favorite in the story is _____. (he, him)
6. Copy out each sentence supplying the correct word in the parentheses. Write whether the correct pronoun is the subject or object pronoun.
7. Lucy told an interesting fable to Rosa and _____. (I, me)
8. _____ is acquainted with the fable. (she, her)
9. According to Mrs. French and _____, Lucy told the story correctly. (she, her)
10. _____ and I taught in the same school. (she, her)
11. The story was modeled on _____. (she, her)

REINFORCEMENT WRITING SENTENCES

1. Write about any topic using as many subject and object pronouns as possible.
2. Write about your best day in school using subject and object pronouns where necessary.

POSSESSIVE PRONOUNS

A possessive pronoun shows ownership. A possessive pronoun can be replaced by a possessive noun.

Dante's Divine Comedy is great.
His Divine Comedy is great.

Be careful of possessive nouns and possessive pronouns that replace them.

Possessive pronouns are identified in two ways, or have two forms. One form is used before a noun; the other form stands alone.

Below is a chart showing the two forms:

Possessive Pronouns			
Used Before Nouns		*Stand Alone*	
My	*Our*	*Mine*	*Ours*
Your	*Your*	*Yours*	*Yours*
His, her, it	*Their*	*His, hers, its*	*Theirs*

Notice the two forms of the possessive pronouns below: the two forms are not used the same way.

This copy of the Iliad is my book. This book is mine.

The copy of the Iliad is your book. This book is yours.

The copy of the Iliad is Mark's book. This book is his.

Possessive pronouns must agree with their antecedent.

He has his own idea about the match. (masculine, singular)

She has _her_ own idea about the match. (feminine, singular)

They discuss _their_ opinions with _their_ classmates.

When a singular indefinite pronoun refers to both males and females, any possessive pronoun in the sentence must indicate this fact.

Each has _his_ or _her_ own opinion about the match.

EXERCISES

A. Copy out each sentence and underline the possessive pronoun. Then write 'before noun' or 'stands alone' to show how the pronoun is used.

1. <u>His</u> life has affected every generation. (before a noun)
2. <u>His</u> name could be found in every age. (before a noun)
3. Nobody possesses a character like his. (stands alone)
4. Many have been affected by him in <u>their</u> lives. (before a noun)
5. <u>Your</u> new film is more interesting than <u>ours</u>. (before a noun; stands alone)

B. Rewrite each sentence; replace each underlined possessive noun with the correct possessive pronoun.

6. The teacher informed us that <u>this class's</u> play this year will be Ananse story.
7. Mrs. Lucas pointed out to Mike that the part of Ananse is <u>Mike's</u>.
8. In the Ananse story, Mr. Anubir talks about Ananse's fascinating mind.
9. Kwaku Ananse appeals to friends to help <u>Ananse</u> gather the world's wisdom.
10. <u>The world's wisdom</u> can never be gathered or measured.

REINFORCEMENT: WRITING SENTENCES

1. Write any narrative employing as many possessive pronouns as possible.
2. Write about any Shakespeare play underlying all of the possessive pronouns.

INDEFINITE PRONOUNS

Unlike indefinite pronouns, most pronouns refer to a specific noun or pronoun/antecedent. Indefinite pronouns do not refer to specific people or things.

No one has been to the playground today.

No one is an indefinite pronoun. It does not refer to any specific noun or pronoun antecedent.

> *An indefinite pronoun is a pronoun that does not refer to any particular person, place or thing.*

Indefinite pronouns are mostly singular forms when they are used as subjects of sentences. Notice the verbs must agree with the singular pronoun.

Everybody loves to sing. Nobody plays football at my school.

Memorize the following:

Singular Indefinite Pronouns			
Anybody	*Either*	*Much*	*One*
Another	*Neither*	*Nothing*	*Each*
Anyone	*Everybody*	*Something*	
No one	*Somebody*	*Someone*	

There are also plural indefinite pronouns. When they are used as the subject of sentences, the verbs must agree with plural pronouns.

Study the following

Plural Indefinite Pronouns		
Both	*Few*	*Many*
Others	*Several*	

Both English students wrote their essay on King Arthur.
Few really remember him in our day.

REFLEXIVE PRONOUNS

When the pronoun reflects the action back to the subject, the pronoun is called a reflexive pronoun.

The lady bought a piano.
The lady bought <u>herself</u> a piano.

Herself is a reflexive pronoun.

In the first sentence, it is not clear whether there were two ladies involved in the buying or just one lady.

In the second sentence, there is no ambiguity.

A reflexive pronoun directs the action back to the subject.

Study this chart of Reflexive Pronouns.

Reflexive Pronouns	
Singular	*Plural*
Myself	*Ourselves*
Yourself	*Yourselves*
Himself, herself, itself	*Themselves*

The reflexive pronouns in the chart above can be used to intensify a statement. In this regard, they are known as intensive pronouns.

Reflexive and intensive pronouns have special usage. They should never be used in place of a subject, pronoun or an object pronoun. An intensive pronoun adds emphasis to a noun or a pronoun that has already been named.

Father made arrangements for our trip.
Father <u>himself</u> made arrangements for our trip.

EXERCISES

A. Copy out each sentence. Fill in the blanks with the correct pronoun or reflexive pronoun in the parentheses.

1. I made _____ an African dish. (me, myself)
2. I purchased _____ a book of African proverbs. (me, myself)
3. The book _____ is a legendary book. (it, itself)
4. My classmates and _____ love to discuss it. (I, myself)
5. Mr. Annubir, the writer _____, loved to talk about it. (him, himself)

B. Fill in the blanks using the correct pronoun in the parentheses.

6. The book _____ was once a textbook. (it, itself)
7. The students, _____, made their own purchases. (they, themselves)
8. We, _____, chose to read the book out loud in class. (our, ourselves)
9. _____ took turns to read it. (we, ourselves)
10. I, _____, particularly loved that book. (myself, me

REINFORCEMENT: WRITING SENTENCES

1. Write five sentences using reflexive pronouns.
2. Write five other sentences using intensive pronouns.

INTERROGATIVE PRONOUNS

Pronouns can be used to ask questions. A pronoun used to ask a question or to interrogate is known as an interrogative pronoun.

Interrogative Pronouns

An interrogative pronoun is a pronoun that is used to introduce an interrogative sentence.

The following are interrogative pronouns:
Who, whom, what, which, and *whose.*

Though *who* and *whom* refer to people, both are used differently. *Who* is used when the interrogative pronoun is the subject of the sentence. *Whom* is used when the interrogative pronoun is the object of the verb or the object of a preposition.

Who introduced the lesson today? (Subject)
Whom does the lesson refer to? (Direct Object)
To whom did you leave the message? (Object of the Preposition)

The interrogative pronouns—which, what, and whose are also used in a special way.

What and *which* usually refer to things and *whose* indicate possessive or ownership.

Books by George Eliot interest me. What interests you?
One of the books is about Falstaff. Which one is it?
I found a copy of Pride and Prejudice. Whose is it?
Some exam papers were left in the book. Whose are they?

Whose is an interrogative pronoun that shows ownership. Be careful not to confuse it with *who's* which is a contraction of *who is.*

EXERCISES

A.   Fill in the blanks with the correct word from the parentheses.

1. _____ is the classroom for these students? (Who, Which)
2. To _____ do they have to report? (who, whom)
3. _____ is the reason for this switch? (Which, What)
4. _____ is to blame, the children or their parents? (Who, Whom)
5. _____ is their homeroom teacher? (Who, Whom)

B.   Fill in the blanks with the correct word from the parentheses.

6. The Iliad is a famous Greek epic poem. _____ wrote it? (who, whom)
7. The Greeks were led in the war by _____? (who, whom)
8. _____ is the hero in this poem? (Who, Whom)
9. _____ wife were the Greeks trying to rescue? (Who's, Whose)
10. The war was between the Greeks and _____? (who, whom)
11. _____ is Areus' son? (Who, Whom)
12. _____ was the reason for Achilles to quit fighting? (What, Who's)
13. _____ was the greatest warrior of the Trojans? (Who, Whom)
14. _____ is your favorite poem of Homer, the Iliad or the Odyssey? (Who, Which)
15. _____ is Paris in the story? (Who, Whose)

REINFORECMENT: WRITING SENTENCES

1. Write ten sentences on any topic using an interrogative pronoun in each sentence.
2. Write about your favorite novel using all the interrogative pronouns you have learned in this lesson.

The Late President Dr. Kwame Nkrumah

REVIEW

Personal Pronouns

A.   Copy out each sentence. Replace the underlined word or words with a pronoun. Indicate whether your choice is a subject pronoun or an object pronoun.

1.   Dr. Kwame Nkrumah helped <u>Ghana</u> achieve her independence.
2.   <u>The country</u> was happy at long last.
3.   <u>Dr. Nkrumah</u> was hailed for his achievement.
4.   <u>The Independence</u> made <u>Dr. Nkrumah</u> very proud.

Pronouns and Antecedents

B.   Fill in the blank with the correct pronoun. Underline the antecedent of the pronoun used.

5.   Accra is the capital of Ghana; _____ has all the parliamentary offices. (it, they)
6.   Ghanaians continue to make progress; _____ have such great faith in God. (it, they)
7.   The football player struggled very hard initially, but _____ finally made it. (he, him)
8.   The new teacher was an African, _____ looked for a fellow African on arrival. (he, him)
9.   The paint was mixed with other colors. _____ matched the existing colors. (it, they)
10. The man was of a different nationality. _____ made acquaintances very quickly. (he, him)

Using Pronouns Correctly

C.   Copy out each sentence using the correct pronoun. Then indicate whether the pronoun you use is a subject pronoun or an object pronoun.

11. _____ Africans are very proud of our heritage. (we, us)
12. It gives _____ a sense of dignity and purpose in life. (it, they, us)
13. It helps _____ relate back to our ancestors. (us, we)

14. Moreover, _____ is a proud and awesome past. (it, they)
15. _____ is so rich and overwhelming, I sometimes wonder if any one person has absorbed a fraction of it. (It, They)
16. My friend and _____ are planning to go to the library for some literature on the subject. (me, I)

Possessive Pronouns

D. Copy out each sentence. Replace the underlined word or words with the correct possessive pronoun.

17. She gained access to the theatre through Joe's help. (him, his)
18. The place was the Greeks'. (theirs, their)
19. They were able to climb to the top by the people's help. (theirs, their)
20. Though late, they were able to stay on for the next session through Mary's kindness. (her, she)

Indefinite Pronouns

E. Fill in the blank with the correct verb in the parentheses. Underline the indefinite pronoun.

21. Several people _____ agreed to attend the rally. (has, have)
22. No one _____ what to do. (know, knows)
23. Nobody _____ in him anymore. (believe, believes)
24. Nothing _____ nowadays. (matter, matters)
25. They both _____ at the office. (work, works)

Reflexive and Intensive Pronouns

F. Fill in the blanks with the correct pronoun in the parentheses.

26. I _____ have read about Hercules. (me, myself)
27. My teacher had briefed _____ on the subject. (us, we)
28. The notes _____ are self explanatory. (themselves, itself)
29. The work _____ is not that hard. (itself, it)
30. The teacher _____ had explained it thoroughly. (herself, she)

Interrogative and Demonstrative Pronouns

G.   Fill in the blanks with the correct pronoun in the parentheses.

31. The Ghana flag has a black star in the middle. _____ does the black star stand for? (what, which)
32. The flag has three colors, red, yellow and green. _____ does the color red stand for? (What, Which)
33. _____ can we count upon to explain the green on the flag? (who, whom)
34. The red represents a people; _____ are the people? (who, whom)
35. The totality of the flag has a meaning; _____ is its significance? (what, which)

ADJECTIVES AND ADVERBS

In this lesson, you are going to learn about adjectives and adverbs. Adjectives describe nouns and pronouns. They describe a person, place, thing, or idea. Adverbs modify verbs, adjectives, and other adverbs.

ADJECTIVES

ADJECTIVE
An adjective is a word that describes a noun or a pronoun.

Our <u>new</u> playground is <u>large</u>.

New and large are adjectives describing playground.

In some cases an adjective appears after a linking verb and describes a noun or a pronoun which is the subject.

The philosopher is <u>brilliant</u> and <u>persuasive</u>.

'Brilliant' and 'persuasive' are predicate adjectives that modify the subject 'philosopher.'

A predicate adjective is an adjective that follows a linking verb. It tells what the subject is like.

PRESENT AND PAST PARTICIPLE

Present and Past Participles can also be used as adjectives and predicate adjectives.

The inhabitants threw an <u>astounding</u> party for the princess.
astounding (present participle)

The Mona Lisa, the <u>painted</u> picture of Leonardo de Vinci, is something to behold.
painted (past participle)

COMPARATIVE AND SUPERLATIVE ADJECTIVES

We learned that adjectives describe nouns and pronouns. Adjectives can also compare two or more nouns or pronouns.

> *The comparative form of an adjective compares two people or things. To form the comparative form of an adjective simply add—er to the adjective.*

> *The superlative form of an adjective compares more than two people or things. To form the superlative form just add—est to the adjective.*

ADJECTIVE	COMPARATIVE	SUPERLATIVE
Tall	Taller	Tallest
Big	Bigger	Biggest
Cold	Colder	Coldest

ADJECTIVE: *Mary is tall. (one person—a girl)*

COMPARATIVE: *Jane is taller than Mary. (two people—two girls)*

SUPERLATIVE: *Sarah is the tallest of the three. (three persons—three girls)*

Some adjectives are different. They are not formed by adding—er or—est. They have special forms and must be memorized.

ADJECTIVE	COMPARATIVE	SUPERLATIVE
Good or well	Better	Best
Bad	Worse	Worst
Many or much	More	Most
Little	Less	Least

EXAMPLES

The weather was <u>bad</u> yesterday.
The weather is <u>worse</u> today.
Tomorrow will be the <u>worst</u> day of all.

EXERCISES

A. Fill in the blanks with the correct adjectives given in the parentheses.

1. Virgil's work is one of the _____ beautiful of all poetry. (much, more, most)
2. Spencer, in his autobiography, tells us about the year of his courtship as being the _____ of all of his forty years. (long, longer, longest)
3. In Homer's The Iliad, the epic starts with the _____ personal quarrel between Achilles and Agammemnon. (less, lesser, least)
4. Agammemnon sends Odyseus, who is considered the _____ of the Greeks. (clever, cleverer, cleverest)
5. Agammemnon was the _____ cantankerous of all the gods. (much, more, most)

B. Fill in the blanks with the correct comparative or superlative form.

6. Dr. Kwame Nkrumah was the first president of Africa and the _____ Chanaian president. (good, better, best)
7. He did the _____ for Ghana in terms of education, health, and its economy. (much, more, most)
8. He had the _____ unusual foresight that was absolutely astounding. (much, more, most)
9. He facilitated the _____ hospital and universities in the nation's capital. (good, better, best)
10. The _____ important public buildings in Accra are the Parliamentary and the Judicial buildings. (much, more, most)

REINFORCEMENT: WRITING SENTENCES

1. Write ten sentences using an adjective that ends in—er or—est.
2. Compare two government buildings using comparative and superlative forms.

Balme Library—University of Ghana, Legon

The Great Hall and Independence Tower, Legon

MORE COMPARATIVE AND SUPERLATIVE

Study the following chart below:

ADJECTIVE	COMPARATIVE	SUPERLATIVE
Serious	More serious	Most serious
Impressive	More impressive	Most impressive
Admirable	More admirable	Most admirable

ADJECTIVE: Ekua drew an impressive picture. (one thing—one picture)

COMPARATIVE: Her latest picture is more impressive than her last picture. (two things—the new, or next picture, and the old, or the last picture)

SUPERLATIVE: Her final picture is the most impressive. (more than two things —the new picture and all of the other pictures)

ADJECTIVE: The onlookers were curious about her picture.

COMPARATIVE: The people were less curious about the old artist's work.

SUPERLATIVE: Of all the Exhibits, the people were the least curious about Kweku Anansi's picture.

Usually a one-syllable adjective takes—er or—est.

An adjective of three or more syllables takes <u>more</u> and <u>most</u> or <u>less</u> and <u>least</u>.

Adjectives with two-syllables vary or differ.

Some two-syllables adjectives take the—er or—est ending. Others take the words <u>more</u> and <u>most</u> or <u>less</u> and <u>least</u>.

Avoid using more or most and less or least before adjectives that are already in the comparative or superlative form. This kind of error is known as a double comparison.

AVOID: The Eburi gardens are the most nicest gardens in the Ashanti district.

CORRECT: The Eburi gardens are the most beautiful gardens in the Ashanti district.

EXERCISES

A. Fill in the blanks with the correct comparative or superlative form given in the parentheses.

1. Netball is one of the _____ women's games in Ghana. (more exciting, most exciting)

2. Good people are _____ about other people's business. (less curious, least curious)

3. Many students find mathematics _____ than other subjects. (more difficult, most difficult)

4. More people have _____ paid jobs nowadays than before. (good, better, best)

5. Pablo Picasso seems to be featured as one of the _____ painters in our time. (good, better, best)

B. Fill the blanks with the correct comparative or superlative form of the adjective given in the parentheses.

6. The buildings in Ghana are _____ than the buildings here. (more elaborate, most elaborate)

7. In my day, the schools in Ghana were _____ than the schools of today. (better organized, best organized)

8. Office work is _____ than masonary work. (less tedious, least tedious)

9. The cocoa farmers in Kumasi found a _____ way to enhance their product. (better, best)

10. During Dr. President Kwame Nkrumah's presidency, the hospitals were _____ than today. (more equipped, better equipped)

REINFORCEMENT:WRITING SENTENCES

1. Write ten sentences using the comparative and superlative froms of the adjectives.
2. Describe a public building in your home town.

DEMONSTRATIVE ADJECTIVES

Demonstrative Adjectives, *this*, *that*, *these*, and *those*, are used as modifiers with nouns or pronouns. They demonstrate or point out specific people, places or things.

EXAMPLES:

1. *I like <u>this</u> table, but I really didn't like <u>that</u> one.*
2. *<u>These</u> cocoa yams are ripe but <u>those</u> white potatoes are no good.*

When demonstrative adjectives are used by themselves and not as modifiers, they are called demonstrative pronouns.

Demonstrative Adjective	*Demonstrative Pronoun*
I love <u>this</u> comedy.	*I know <u>this</u>.*
We saw <u>that</u> play.	*We have <u>that</u>.*

USING DEMONSTRATIVE ADJECTIVES

Use *<u>this</u>* and *<u>that</u>* with singular nouns. Use *<u>these</u>* and *<u>those</u>* with plural nouns.

This flower	*These flowers*
That basket	*Those baskets*

Avoid using the object pronoun 'them' in place of the demonstrative adjective 'those.'

CORRECT:	I cleaned those shelves.
AVOID:	I cleaned them shelves.

<u>Kind</u> and <u>sort</u> are singular nouns.

Therefore, it is right to say *<u>this</u>* kind and *<u>this</u>* sort.

For plurals we say these kinds and those. *<u>These</u>* and *<u>those</u>* are used only with the plural: *<u>these</u> kinds or <u>those</u> sorts.*

EXERCISES

A.   Fill in the blanks with the correct word or words in the parentheses.

1. _____ is the time of year the fishes migrate. (This, That)
2. _____ is the meadow where the animals feed. (This, That)
3. _____ are the playgrounds where the children play after school. (These, Those)
4. _____ is the field where the farmers use to graze their cattle. (This, That)
5. They have a good season this year. _____ is why they are planting early. (This, That)

B   Fill in the blanks with the correct word given in parentheses.

6. _____ beautiful school was built only recently. (This, That)
7. The grown-ups saw _____ things in a new perspective. (those, these)
8. These _____ paintings have become attractive to the youth. (kinds of, kind of)
9. _____ is not the _____ art work that will appeal to grown-ups. (This, These) (sort of, sorts of)
10. _____ painting by Monet has attracted many. (That, Those, These)

REINFOREMENT: WRITING SENTENCES

Write ten sentences on one of the following topics. Use *this, that, these,* and *those* as demonstrative adjectives in some of your sentences as well as demonstrative pronouns in others.

1. Write about a visit to an art gallery.
2. Write about one of the famous artists whose work really captures the audience.

ADVERBS

We learned that an adjective is a word that describes a noun or a pronoun. An adverb is another kind of word that often describes an action verb. An action verb always names an action.

The choir sings <u>gloriously</u> at Easter and Christmas.

The word <u>gloriously</u> in the above sentence describes the action word 'sings.'

The referee cancelled the game <u>quite</u> suddenly.

The game was held in a <u>very</u> tight stadium.

In the first sentence, the adverb <u>suddenly</u> describes the verb <u>cancelled</u> and the adverb <u>quite</u> describes the adverb <u>suddenly</u>.

In the second sentence, the adverb <u>very</u> describes the adjective <u>tight</u>.

> *An adverb is a word that modifies or describes a verb, an adjective or another adverb.*

The following sentences will explain the work of an adverb:

The early chapters of the book <u>effectively</u> aroused the feelings and sensibilities of the students.

Many readers are <u>always</u> trying to capture the poet's mind.

Many young readers are always trying to see themselves <u>there</u> in the poet's mind.

An adverb may explain how or in what manner the action is done. It may also explain when and how often the action is done. It may show where or in what direction the action took place.

COMMON ADVERBS		
How? (in what manner)	*When?* (how often)	*Where?* (in what direction)
Peacefully	*Once; sometimes*	*Forward; backward*
Heroically	*Daily*	*Everywhere; here*
Bravely	*Often*	*Have; nearby*
Patiently	*Always*	*Across*

When an adverb describes a verb, you will see that the adverb appears in different places.

The contractor carefully studies the map from the architect.

The contractor studies the map <u>carefully</u> from the architect.

<u>Carefully</u>, the contractor studies the map from the architect.

CONTRACTIONS

A contraction is made up of two words that are combined into one word and usually omitting one or two letters.

An apostrophe (') is used in a contraction to show that one or more letters have been omitted.

The word <u>not</u> employed in a sentence can alter the entire meaning of the sentence from a positive statement to a negative one.

Study the chart below:

Words	Contractions
Is not	*Isn't*
Was not	*Wasn't*
Were not	*Weren't*
Do not	*Don't*
Did not	*Didn't*
Have not	*Haven't*
Had not	*Hadn't*
Will not	*Won't*
Would not	*Wouldn't*
Should not	*Shouldn't*

Notice that in all but two of these words, the apostrophe replaces the 'o' in not. In can't both the 'o' and the 'n' are omitted. Will not changes to won't.

The word 'not' is a negative word.

Below are some other negative words:

No	Scarcely
Never	Barely
None	Hardly
Nobody	Rarely
No one	But (when used as a negative)
Nothing	Only (when used as a negative)

Avoid using double negative or two negatives together.

CORRECT: *The indigenous Africans built no elaborate structures.*

CORRECT: *The indigenous Africans didn't build any elaborate structures.*

AVOID: *The indigenous Africans didn't build no elaborate structures.*

The last sentence has two negative words, or a double negative, which should be avoided. Only one negative word is necessary.

EXERCISES

A. Copy out each sentence and fill in the blanks with the correct word in the parentheses.

1. Bad behavior among children _____ common in many parts of the world. (was, wasn't)

2. There was no way kids _____ act up in rural areas. (could, couldn't)

3. In the past, bad behavior _____ a problem for many parents. (was, wasn't)

4. Children _____ never dream of the things the teens are doing nowadays. (would, wouldn't)

5. In Africa, one _____ always correct any kid. (would, wouldn't)

B. Write the contractions of the following.

6. is not
7. cannot
8. will not
9. must not
10. were not
11. did not
12. do not
13. was not
14. are not
15. am not
16. has not

C. Fill in the blanks using the correct word or words given in the parentheses.

17. Before President Kwame Nkrumah took office, no one in the village _____ ever thought about going to school. (had, hadn't)

18. Until then, the village kids _____ no idea about schooling. (had, hadn't)

19. Now the idea of going to school _____ entered the minds of rural children. (has, hasn't)

20. It is a pity that education is _____ free. (no longer, any longer)

21. No one ever thought kids _____ to pay fees to go to school. (would have, wouldn't have)

22. _____ a big struggle for poor parents to have to pay fees. (It is, Isn't)

REINFORCEMENT: WRITING SENTENCES

Write ten sentences on one of the following topics using contractions.

1. **Say how you would encourage your government to make education free for all.**
2. **Explain how free education benefits the poor.**

ACCRA - GHANA

INTENSIFIERS

An adverb that emphasizes or intensifies an adjective, or an adverb is called an in tensifier.

> The natives of Easter Island constructed massive statues.

> The natives of Easter Island constructed extremely massive statues.

In the first sentence, the natives constructed massive statues. The adjective massive describes the noun 'statues.' In the second sentence, we are told that, the statues are extremely massive. The intensifier extremely describes the adjective 'massive.'

Below are some examples:

> Visitors love to look at really fascinating statues.

> Visitors love to look at statues prayerfully.

> Some visitors love to look at statues rather thoughtfully.

REVIEW

A. __ADJECTIVES__: Copy out each sentence. Draw a line under each adjective and draw an arrow to the noun it describes. Then circle any predicate adjective you may find.

1. Our African forefathers made durable huts that could test the times.
2. The amazing huts showed interesting features.
3. Modern people have inherited these huts since olden days.
4. Fascinating work had been done along the inner walls.

B. __ARTICLES AND PROPER ADJECTIVES__: Copy down each group of words. Capitalize and underline each proper adjective. Then put the correct indefinite article before each group of words.

5. new accra stadium
6. delicious african dish
7. fascinating french art
8. unusual european couple
9. wholesome english muffin
10. good irish class

C. __COMPARATIVE AND SUPERLATIVE ADJECTIVES__: Copy down each sentence using the correct comparative or superlative adjective form in the parentheses.

11. I think the _____ building in Accra is Job 600. (impressive, most impressive)
12. It was _____ than any other building when it was first built. (popular, more popular)
13. The size is one of the _____ of the government buildings. (most largest, largest)

D. __DEMONSTRATIVE ADJECTIVES__: Fill in the blanks with the correct word or words from the parentheses.

14. My friend made _____ outfits. (those, them)
15. _____ dress hanging in the window is typical of her work. (This, This here)
16. Is _____ dress on the rack one of hers too? (that, that there)

17. The design of _____ wedding dresses was influenced by her. (those, them)

18. Her style resembles _____ of a factory outlet. (those, them)

E.   ADVERBS AND INTENSIFIERS: Copy out each sentence. Underline each adverb once and each intensifier twice. Then indicate whether it describes an action verb, an adverb, or an adjective.

19. Contractors work seriously on their building.

20. Many contractors very often make a new design.

21. They work together with one aim in mind.

22. A well-built house meets the satisfaction of the owner fully.

23. A truly ambitious architect seriously aims at creating a really new design.

F.   COMPARATIVE AND SUPERLATIVE ADVERBS: Write down the comparative and superlative forms of each adverb.

24. Good

25. Long

26. Far (distance)

27. Far (degree)

28. Slow

29. Intensely

30. Effectively

31. Friendly

G.   AVOIDING DOUBLE NEGATIVES: Fill in the blanks with the correct word or words from the parentheses.

32. Scarcely _____ comes to the games without something in hand to wave. (anyone, no one)

33. I have _____ seen people anywhere who would give up everything for games. (never, ever)

34. There is hardly _____ spectator who would sit still when a goal is about to be scored. (any, no)

35. One _____ hardly believe the behavior of some spectators at a match game. (can, can't)

UNIT REVIEW

PRONOUNS

A.   Copy out each sentence and fill in the blanks with the correct pronoun that agrees with the underlined antecedent.

1.   Books about famous Ghanaians are available in the library; many past students have read _____them. (Books about famous Ghanaian)

2.   My friend has read one or two of these books. She finds_____very fascinating. them. (these books)

3.   The young Ghanaian should be encouraged to read about such notable people as Efua Sauderland, Pa Grant, Dr. Danquah,Caseley Hayford and Mensah Sarbah to mention just a few. The children will learn a lot from_____.them (notable people).

4.   These books include the autobiography of the Late Dr. Kwame Nkrumah. Do You know about him. (the late Dr. Kwame Nkrumah)

5.   These great people's _____ could be found in the archives. their (names

B.   Underline the correct word or words in the parentheses.

1.   Gloria read a poem by Shelly to (her and me, she and I).

2.   Grace and (I, me) both love Shakespeare.

3.   (Its, It's) her favorite book.

4.   That book on the shelf is not mine but (hers, her's)

5.   We read about the Frog and Lizard. The only known characters in the book are (they, them).

6.   (Her and I, She and I, Her and me) acted out a scene for our class.

C.   Fill in the blanks with the correct word given in the parentheses.

7.   (Who's, Whose) copy of the magazine is this?

8.   Someone left (her, their) copy in the lunchroom.

9.   Everyone (has, had) read some of the assigned stories.

10.   I bought (me, myself) a copy of the magazine.

11.   Elizabeth and (I, myself) read the stories.

12.   Few can choose (his, her,their) favorite character from these stories.

PREPOSITIONS, CONJUNCTIONS AND INTERJECTIONS

In this chapter, you are going to learn about two ways of connecting words. One, you will learn how prepositions relate nouns or pronouns to other words in sentences; and two, you will learn how conjunctions connect words, phrases or other parts of sentences. You will also learn about interjections. Interjections are words that express strong feelings.

PREPOSITIONS AND PREPOSITIONAL PHRASES

> *A proposition is a word that relates a noun or a pronoun to another word.*

The picture against the wall is mine.

In the above sentence, the word *against* is a preposition.

Memorize the following prepositions:

Aboard	*Before*	*During*	*Toward*
About	*Behind*	*Except*	*Under*
Above	*Below*	*For*	*Underneath*
Across	*Beneath*	*From*	*Until*
After	*Beside*	*In*	*Up*
Against	*Between*	*Inside*	*Upon*
Along	*Beyond*	*Into*	*With*
Among	*By*	*Like*	
At	*Down*	*Of*	

Some prepositions consist of more than one word.

Instead of	According to	Aside from
In place of	Across from	Because of
In front of	On account of	

Below is an example of a *prepositional phrase*.

President Kwame Nkrumah hails <u>from a small town</u>.

The group of words, *<u>from a small town</u>*, is called a prepositional phrase.

A prepositional phrase is a group of words that begins with a preposition and ends with a noun or a pronoun. The noun or pronoun is known as *<u>the object of the preposition</u>*.

EXERCISES

A. Copy out each sentence. Then underline the prepositional phrase and circle the preposition.

1. Some African Heads of State look at President Kwame Nkrumah for inspiration.
2. His legacy had a great influence on many other Heads of State.
3. Many people in Ghana see insights in his work.
4. Successive presidents have tried to follow his footsteps.
5. Dr. Kwame Nkrumah was admired by many Heads of State outside Ghana.
6. Many modern individuals have been influenced by Dr. Kwame Nkrumah.
7. He designed new roads in a very short time.
8. He helped the Tema community to come alive within a very short time.
9. One could say Dr. Nkrumah changed Ghana over night.
10. Other presidents, outside Ghana, had looked to Kwame Nkrumah as a man of foresight.

REINFORCEMENT: WRITING SENTENCE

1. Write ten sentences using prepositional phrases and circle the preposition.
2. Write about any favorite individual using prepositional phrases.

PREPOSITIONAL PHRASES AS ADJECTIVES AND ADVERBS

The function of a prepositional phrase is to describe the work of a word or group of words that shows up in the same sentence. When a prepositional phrase is used to describe a noun, the phrase functions as an adjective.

Those <u>enormous</u> statues are quite magnificent.

Those statues <u>from the Vatican</u> are quite magnificent.

In the first sentence above, the adjective *enormous* describes the noun *statues*. In the second sentence, the prepositional phrase *from the Vatican* describes statues. The phrase *from the Vatican* works as an adjective.

An adjectival phrase is a prepositional phrase that modifies, or describes, a noun or pronoun.

Sometimes, an adjectival phrase describes a noun in the subject part of the sentence. Other times, it may describe a noun in the predicate part.

These rugs <u>from the north</u> are old.

These old rugs are rugs <u>from the north</u>.

A prepositional phrase can also work as an adverb describing a verb. An adverbial phrase shows how, when, and where an action takes place.

> *An adverbial phrase is a prepositional phrase that modifies or describes a verb.*

Notice that each adverbial phrase shown below describes the action of the verb.

Students are very quiet in the morning. (When?)

They work quietly. (How?)

They work in different classroom setting. (Where?)

Sometimes the same prepositional phrase works in twofold as an adjective in one sentence and as an adverb in another.

The paint <u>on the wall</u> is very thick. (adjectival phrase)

The paint shines <u>on the wall</u>. (adverbial phrase)

In the first sentence, <u>*on the wall*</u> describes the noun <u>*paint*</u>. In the second sentence, <u>*on the wall*</u> describes the verb shine.

A young Ghanaian weaving kente cloth

**Dr. Nana Kobina Nketsia IV, Vice Chancellor of the University
of Ghana, offering a strip of Kente cloth to Dr. W.E.B. Dubois
during his stay in Ghana.**

EXERCISES

A.   Copy out each sentence. Underline each prepositional phrase. Then write whether it is an adjectival phrase or an adverbial phrase.

1.   African weavers in the whole African continent imitated an old skill.
2.   The very first weavers wove with long grass strands or raffia.
3.   The weavers in ancient Africa learned new skills as they progressed.
4.   African weavers today employ a diversity of colorful raffia.
5.   Ancient carvings on walls indicate that weaving had evolved many centuries ago.

B.   Copy down each sentence. Underline each prepositional phrase once. Underline the word it describes twice. Then indicate whether the prepositional phrase is an adjectival phrase or an adverbial phrase.

6.   A large number of people have shown a longing for this craft.
7.   The Ashantis weave on narrow beautiful strips.
8.   The young apprentice often starts with an old easy pattern.
9.   Old patterns from way back help teach the skills.
10. A whole woven piece by one individual may be worth a lot.
11. Kente cloth with elaborate designs fills Ghana markets.
12. These designs always tell stories about great kings.

REINFORCEMENT: WRITING SENTENCES

Write ten sentences on one of the following topics.

1.   What you know about any weaving industry using adjectival and adverbial phrases. Indicate which phrases are adjectival and which ones are adverbial.
2.   Write about your favorite pastime using adverbial and adjectival phrases.

ADINKRA CLOTH

Adinkra Designs

History has it that Adinkra was the name of a very famous king who hailed from Gyaman, the present day Ivory Coast. It is believed that, Adinkra had a feud with Bonsu-Panin, the Ashantihene, because he attempted to copy the Ashanti Golden Stool. A battle ensued during which Adinkra was defeated. It is also believed that the Adinkra Art originated from Gyaman. The name Adinkra means farewell -- strictly speaking, the farewell was intended to bid good-bye to the deceased king, the famous Adinkra-- hence the creation of the Adinkra cloth. The Adinkra, therefore is a funeral cloth; it comes only in black and red-brown with glossy black designs.

Below are some symbols of the Adinkra cloth:

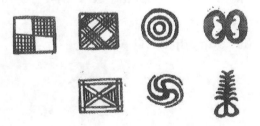

Key

 Adinkrahene (Adinkra king).
Chief of all the adinkra designs, forms the basis of adinkra printing.

 Nkonsonkonson (link or chain)
We are linked in both life and death. Those who share common, blood relations never break apart. Symbol of human relations.

 Kodee mmowerewa (the talons of the eagle). This is also said to be shaved on the heads of some court attendants.

 Aya (the fern).
This word also means 'I am not afraid of you.' A symbol of defiance.

 Nhwimu (crossing). The divisions done onto the plain cloth before the stamping is done.

 Mframadan (wind house).
House built to stand windy and treacherous conditions.

 Kontire ne Akwam (elders of the state).
"Tikoro mmpam" (one head does not constitute a council).

CONJUNCTIONS

A conjunction is a word that joins words or groups of words together.

A coordinating conjunction is a word used to connect parts of a sentence namely words or phrases. The following words *and, but, or, for,* and *nor* are used as coordinating conjunctions.

A coordinating conjunction can be used to join two subjects, two predicates, two objects of a preposition, or two sentences.

Mary or Elizabeth worked at our school. (compound subject)

William studied philosophy and taught it. (compound predicate)

Singing interests you and me. (compound object of preposition)

Some old African mothers were never educated, but their wisdom is quite outstanding. (compound sentence)

A comma is used before a coordinating conjunction that joins the two simple sentences together in a compound sentence.

<u>Yet</u> and <u>so</u> are not coordinating conjunction by themselves except when they are used with *and*.

Renee loves opera, and so she often goes to the Opera House.

> *Correlative conjunctions are pairs of words that are used to connect parts of a sentence.*

<u>Both</u> the Renaissance <u>and</u> the Enlightenment played a key role in shaping the world.

Common Correlative Conjunctions		
Both . . . and	*Neither . . . nor*	*Either . . . or*
Not only . . . but also	*Whether . . . or*	*Just as . . . so*

When a compound subject is joined by the conjunction *and*, the subject is plural. The verb, therefore, must agree with the plural.

Theresa and Ann are world swimmers.

When a compound subject is joined by *or* or *nor*, the verb has to agree with the nearer simple subject.

Neither the two brothers nor Josephine is a good match.

The concert is either this weekend or next weekend.

EXERCISES

A. Copy out each sentence and underline the conjunction. Then indicate whether the conjunction joins a compound subject, compound predicate, compound object of a preposition, or compound sentence.

1. The baker added more water, for she desired the right consistency.
2. The baker owned a part of the bakery, and worked there on special occasions.
3. Both a fish-monger and a butcher require a well-ventilated work area.
4. The teacher attended several workshops, but students now study under her.
5. The students and their parents visited the museum.

B. Fill in the blanks using the correct verb from the parentheses.

6. Neither the students nor their teacher _____ today. (comes, come)
7. Both the drawing and the painting _____ priceless. (is, are)
8. The painter and the sculptor _____ the same studio. (shares, share)
9. The principal and the teacher _____ different ideas. (have, has)
10. Watercolors or oils _____ sometimes used too. (is, are)

REINFORCEMENT: WRITING SENTENCES

Write ten sentences on one of the following topics using correlative and coordinating conjunctions.

1. Describe a special exhibition in which you took part.
2. Imagine that you are a critic at any interesting show. Give your comments.

INTERJECTIONS

We learned at the very beginning the different types of sentences, one being the exclamatory sentence which expresses strong feelings. Sometimes we express strong feelings in a short exclamation that is not a complete sentence. These exclamations are called *interjections*. Below are some common interjections.

My Goodness	Yippee	Zowie
Aha	Oops	Hey

An interjection is a word or group of words that express strong feelings. An interjection does not have any grammatical function in the sentence.

Below are some examples of interjections:

We are going to the Royal Festival Hall. Yippee!

Gee, the public library is closed today.

An interjection that occurs at the start of a sentence is followed by a comma. When an interjection stands alone, it is necessary to put an exclamation mark at the end.

EXERCISES

Copy out each sentence, and underline the interjection.

1. My! I have never heard anybody who could sing so high.
2. Golly, I hope she would sign my card for me.
3. It is certainly a headache to watch those youngsters in a park. Phew!
4. It is likely you will meet the young pop singer. Hooray!
5. Wow! The light from the morning sun is hurting the new growth.
6. I was going to stay a little longer; however, my ride is here, alas.
7. Oh, I am going to be late for my singing lesson.

REINFORCEMENT: WRITING SENTENCES

Write ten sentences on anyone of the following topics using an interjection in each sentence.

1. Describe your first visit to a concert hall and what it did for you.
2. Describe a motion picture you have seen.

FINDING ALL THE PARTS OF SPEECH

Each word in a sentence has its grammatical function. Each word belongs to a category called a part of speech. The part of speech of a word depends on its grammatical function it performs in the sentence.

<u>Parts of Speech</u>

Noun   names a person, place, thing, or idea.

Verb   names an action (action verb) or tells what a subject is or is like (linking verb).

Pronoun   takes the place of one or more nouns.

Adjective   describes a noun or a pronoun.

Adverb   describes a verb, an adjective, or another adverb.

Preposition   relates a noun or a pronoun to another word.

Interjection   expresses strong feeling.

Conjunction   connects words or group of words.

My! She is clever and works skillfully with raffia.

Word	Part of Speech	Reason
My	Interjection	Expresses strong feeling
She	Pronoun	Takes the place of a noun
Is	Linking verb	Tells what she is like
Clever	Adjective	Describes she
And	Conjunction	Joins is clever and works skillfully with raffia
Works	Action verb	Names an action
Skillfully	Adverb	Describe the verb works
With	Preposition	Relates works and raffia
Raffia	Noun	Names a thing

REINFORCEMENT: WRITING SENTENCES

Write ten sentences on anyone of the topics below. Use all the parts of speech and label each one accordingly.

1. Write about a popular museum in your hometown.
2. Write about any sculptor you know.